Wild Splendors of California

Wild Splendors of California

Lalo Fiorelli

Editor: Lalo Fiorelli
Editorial Assistant: Katey O'Neill
Graphic Design and Production: Katey O'Neill
Published in Soquel, California
Printed in Hong Kong

Library of Congress Control Number: 2001127189

ISBN 0-9717228-1-1

ISBN 0-9717228-0-3

Front Cover: *Curving road, west Walker River.*
Back Cover: *"Full flaps." (Immature snow goose.)*
Half-Title Page: *Canada geese at sunrise, Mount Shasta.*
Title Page: *"Big wind." (Kelso Dunes, Mojave Desert.)*

Contents

Introduction   Page vii

Underwater   1
CHANNEL ISLANDS NATIONAL MARINE SANCTUARY   2
MONTERY BAY NATIONAL MARINE SANCTUARY   6

Deserts   17
ANZA BORREGO DESERT STATE PARK   18
MOJAVE DESERT   30
DEATH VALLEY NATIONAL MONUMENT   40

Coastal Range   49
FALL   50
WINTER   56
SPRING   66

Mountains and Valleys   73
SOUTHERN SEQUOIA   74
MONO LAKE   80
BODIE   84
TOIYABE NATIONAL FOREST   90

Wildlife Refuges   97
LOWER KLAMATH LAKE   98
TULE LAKE   112
SACRAMENTO NATIONAL WILDLIFE REFUGE   116

Volcano!   125
BOLAM GLACIER   126

The Photography   130

Vocalizing bull elephant seal.

Introduction

Wild Splendors of California is the result of my many-year love affair with California's wild places, and my desire to share the beauty I have found with you. These images of natural history environments within California show the great biological and geological diversity of the state in a single forum. No image is of a chance encounter with a particular environment. Rather, all are the result of going back to these wonderful places several times over many years and experiencing a variety of seasonal and climatic conditions.

Wild Splendors of California is a photographic essay that tours the state from south to north, from the underwater canyons of the Carmel trench to the volcanic peaks of the southern Cascades. California contains most of the geological features that exist on the planet. Presented here are images from underwater in the intertidal zone, coastal redwood "rain forests," deserts, alpine forests, the mighty Sierra Nevadas running along the spine of the state, national wildlife refuges that protect the Pacific Flyway, and Mount Shasta.

I have written about wilderness areas where, thankfully, ecological and environmental conditions have actually improved over the last few decades. I have avoided making the book academic; there are few Latin botanical/biological names used, and the histories are more anecdotal than factual. Within the text, I use both "I" and "we," depending on the particular circumstances of the experience being related. Although most photos have purely descriptive captions (in italics), there are a few images that are given playful "pet" names that appear within quotes.

Many people helped along the way by providing information and sometimes access to places not normally visited. Without their help *Wild Splendors of California* could not include such diverse habitats. I would like to thank Thom Sutfin, manager of the Soquel Demonstration State Forest; ranger Chuck Bancroft of Point Lobos State Reserve; ranger Tom Vandenberg of the Klamath Basin National Wildlife Refuges; and Kevin Merk, bio/botanist and good friend, who gave much of his time and knowledge identifying species. I have great praise for and give my wholehearted thanks to graphic designer Katey O'Neill; she was able to successfully take my vision and translate it into book form. The most important individual to thank is my spouse, Evy Cambridge. She has been with me on almost all my field trips for the last 15 years. Evy also did all my remote lighting in the Underwater section. She is a major source of inspiration for me.

—Lalo Fiorelli

Underwater

The ocean! Although water covers over 70% of the planet, the underwater realm is a place where relatively few human beings have ventured, despite the increasing popularity of scuba diving.

The subaquatic regions presented here lie within the intertidal zones of the California mainland coast and the Channel Islands. Diving conditions are challenging. Water temperatures are relatively cold with winter temperatures as low as 46 degrees Fahrenheit. Divers venturing into these waters on a regular basis invariably give up wet suits in favor of dry suits with heavy insulating layers. In water temperature this cold, a diver will find that the exposed part of the face around the mask stings at first contact. Unlike the typical tropical water visibility in calm, warm water of from 60 to 100 feet, in these regions 30 feet visibility is more the norm, 60 feet very unusual, and 15 feet or less is quite common. Add to this the tremendous energy of the Pacific Ocean as it comes near the land, and you have a mix of conditions that keeps most divers away.

As one descends into the ocean, all the vibrant colors visible on the surface disappear by 35 feet. Your world becomes monochromatic blues and greens. It is only when an artificial light source is played over the underwater landscape that a riot of color becomes visible. The colors rival the most beautiful of nature's adornments anywhere in the world.

Above: Rose anenome.
Opposite: Ling cod.

Channel Islands National Marine Sanctuary

The Channel Islands are a group of islands ranging from 11 to 65 miles offshore from the southern California coast. They encompass six major islands from San Clemente in the south to San Miguel in the north. San Miguel is slightly southwest of Santa Barbara, and San Clemente is offshore of its namesake city of San Clemente, between Los Angeles and San Diego. The islands are arrayed over 175 miles of ocean.

The Channel Islands National Marine Sanctuary is the oldest National Marine Sanctuary in the U.S. It extends six nautical miles offshore from each island, excluding San Clemente Island which is not part of the sanctuary. It was created by a very forward-thinking group of people at a time when awareness of the necessity to protect our ocean environment was in its infancy. It became the model and impetus for all the marine sanctuaries that followed.

These images were shot in the depths off the islands of Santa Cruz, Santa Rosa, and San Miguel. San Miguel, the most northwesterly and exposed of the islands, has the most interesting topography underwater, with large pinnacles and rock walls extending hundreds of feet up from the ocean floor. Due to its exposure to the northwest swells of the open ocean originating somewhere in the Aleutian island chain, San Miguel frequently is undiveable.

On a trip to San Miguel one fall, the ocean was tranquil and we were able to spend 3 days diving the exposed side of the island. Sites with such names as Wilson's Rock, Sky Scrapers, and Castle Rock all conjure memories for me of very early morning dives to take advantage of the extraordinarily calm ocean conditions we were lucky enough to encounter. These are considered advanced dives, at the limits of sport diving. The water was pristine due to the remoteness of the sites and exposure to thousands of miles of open ocean.

The underwater pinnacles have vertical walls covered with great areas of scallops and colonies of many different species of anemone. In some areas dense concentrations of red abalone are present. When we first came upon such an abundance of abalone, we couldn't believe what we were seeing. Fish were also present in great numbers. Large sheepshead were common, as were red rockfish, large schools of blue fish, and angel sharks which are relatively common on sandy bottoms. We also sighted an occasional blue shark.

Sea cucumbers.

Giant kelp.

Above: Puffball sponges.

Right: Seahares mating.

Monterey Bay National Marine Sanctuary

POINT LOBOS STATE RESERVE

When Robert Louis Stevenson visited Point Lobos in 1879, he was so inspired by the landscape that he used it as the basis for the setting of his novel *Treasure Island*. The original Spanish name of the site was *Punta de los Lobos Marinos,* or Point of the Wolves of the Sea, named for the large numbers of California sea lions present.

Point Lobos was established as a State Reserve in the early 1930s, 700 protected acres of it being underwater; no plant or animal life of any kind may be molested or taken from these waters. The underwater portion of the reserve includes Whaler's Cove (the site of an old whaling outpost) and Bluefish Cove and extends out from land to near the edge of the Carmel Trench.

Because of its long-time protected status, and due in part to the cold, nutrient-rich waters that well up from the depths of the Carmel Trench, Point Lobos is one of the richest marine habitats in California. Standing on the rocky shore of outer Whaler's Cove, one sees the tops of rock walls and pinnacles that extend from above water down to the ocean floor 60 to 100 feet below. Underwater, these walls have an incredible diversity of marine life growing on and swimming around them.

Growing on the walls are *Corynactus,* vivid red colonial anenomes with white clubbed arms. The colonies actually carpet whole areas of the walls. Other non-colonial anenomes, such as the northern red and giant green, exhibit unbelievable color combinations. And fish! It seems like the fish understand they are protected in the reserve. On any given day you will probably see lingcod, cabezon, blue fish, red rock fish (commonly called snapper but not in the same family), and many other rock fish too numerous to mention. There are a variety of sharks including, on very rare occasions, the great white. Sheepshead and occasionally ocean sun fish, also known as *mola mola,* are seen in the reserve. There are a variety of rays, including the Pacific electric ray. These rays are quite docile and will allow approach—but beware! If touched gently, you will feel a light electric shock, even through neoprene gloves, despite not upsetting or agitating the ray.

A major feature in Whaler's Cove is the giant kelp. During the summer months it grows at the rate of over a foot a day. The view for divers is breathtaking when looking up from the bottom during periods of good underwater visibility. The kelp extends 90 feet from the bottom to the surface, and a diver looking up from the ocean floor gets the same feeling as being in a majestic conifer forest with sunlight streaming through the canopy.

Corynactus anenomes.

Mouth of northern red anenome.

Starfish arm and chestnut cowry.

Hydracoral, Carmel Trench.

"Sea creature with flower in her hair." (Rose anenome on encrusted rock.)

MONTEREY BAY PROPER

Monterey Bay is a portion of the immense area protected by inclusion in the Monterey Bay National Marine Sanctuary. The Sanctuary was created in the early 1990s. The bay itself was once one of the most heavily polluted coastal bodies of water in the United States due to the heavy pesticide runoff from agriculture conducted near streams and rivers draining into it. Since the banning of some toxic pesticides and restrictions on fishing and harvesting of other underwater resources, the submarine aspect of the bay has recovered a great deal of its former health and beauty.

Most of the diving done in Monterey Bay is in the waters adjacent to the Monterey peninsula, from the breakwater to Point Pinos. The breakwater, on the very inside of the bay, is the most protected. The bottom here is quite barren and muddy. However, at a depth of 70 feet there is a small outcropping of rock that is home to a colony of *Metritium* anenomes. These anenomes are quite tall, adults having stalks of over one foot in length and feeding apparatus around one foot in diameter. They have a translucent, creamy appearance, and when fully extended their tops appear very lacy. Looking carefully while diving beside the rock fill that makes up the breakwater, we were rewarded with sightings of many different animals: brittlestars, other starfish, nudibranchs, sea slugs, a variety of small rock fish, turban snails, and an occasional lingcod.

It is here in the early days of my diving that I first encountered the playful nature of the California sea lion. One of these wonderful animals grabbed hold of my fin and gave it a yank. He wanted to play! We cavorted for the next ten minutes, doing underwater acrobatics together. If I did a loop, he did one. When I did a roll, he imitated me. We repeated these maneuvers together many times. When my air supply was getting low and I turned to swim away, he once again grabbed hold of my fin and yanked. Truly, he didn't want me to leave! What a joy it was to interact with this wild creature in his native habitat.

The dive sites along this side of the peninsula have names from Monterey's Cannery Row days. Lover's Point is one such site. Names of other dive sites that are all near the old Cannery Row are The Breakwater, Chase Reef, and the Point Pinos Light at the very end of the peninsula. Frequently we have been turned back from attempting to dive at Point Pinos by the strong wave conditions.

Once, upon surfacing from a dive at Lover's Point, I found myself two feet from a California sea otter. I had heard a funny tapping noise as I was surfacing that I couldn't figure out. An otter was lying on his back using a rock to break the shell of an abalone. Perhaps because I had come from underwater this otter decided I was no threat. He looked me in the eye and then continued the business of feeding.

Metritium anenome.

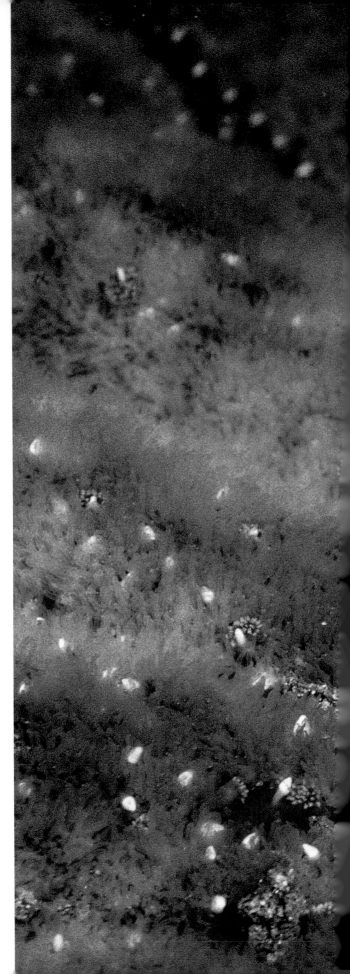

Above: Nudibranch egg case.

*Right: Black eye gobi
on sunstar back.*

 Deserts

In California lie the hottest, lowest, and most sparsely populat~~ed~~ the Great American Deserts. In the early days of California m~~igra~~tion, these lands struck fear in the hearts of travelers. They we~~re~~ places to be crossed in as short a time as possible with hopes ~~of~~ minimum loss of life.

Many species once thrived here during the time when the cl~~imate~~ was more hospitable. As the climate became more arid, some adapted and survived while others became extinct. The fossil~~s~~ of the California deserts date, in some instances, to three mil~~lion~~ years old. There is evidence of man living here as long as 21~~,000~~ years ago.

Today our deserts teem with an incredible diversity of plant ~~and~~ animal life. Both plants and animals have developed physiologi~~es~~ to not only survive but thrive in these arid lands. In many cases simi~~lar~~ characteristics and similar animal characteristics developed through convergent evolution as living organisms adapted over time to the desert environment.

I love the desert. When I am in the desert, I feel an incredible peace come over me. It becomes easy to remember who I am.

~~opposite:~~
Eureka Dunes.

Left:Barrel cactus landscape, with ocotillo.

Below: Barrel cactus spines.

Inside a barrel cactus bloom.

Desert asters, Split Mountain.

Desert primrose.

Above: Ocotillo blooms.

Right: "Perfect camouflage." (Western diamondback rattlesnake in creekside brush.)

View from Font's Point.

Rock swirls, Split Mountain.

Above: Agaves in bloom.

Left: Agave plants.

Weather-eroded sandstone.

Mojave Desert

That the Mojave is vast is a true understatement. The portion of the Mojave protected by the California Desert Protection Act of 1994 alone is 1.4 million acres. This area is called the Mojave National Preserve and exists in the heart of the Mojave Desert. Within the National Preserve are 22 areas designated as "wilderness." Two other vast desert areas meet the Mojave: the Great Basin to the north and east and the Sonora Desert to the south. Sand dunes, volcanic cinder cones, desert scrub land, mountain-top forests, and the mighty Colorado River on the eastern border of California are all part of the Mojave Desert landscape.

Evidence exists of people having lived in this desert as early as ten thousand years ago. Rock art throughout the desert points to a long history of human presence. Relatively recent human activities have left their mark on the desert in the form of old mines, abandoned ranches, and signs of the era of steam locomotives. The Kelso railroad depot was abandoned and boarded up after the demise of steam locomotives. The depot was built in 1924 to service the steam engines that made the steep climb up Cima Grade. The depot was not officially closed until 1985. There are plans to restore it. Hopefully it will someday return to its former grandeur.

In the Whipple Mountains in the southeastern corner of the Mojave, just north of Parker Dam, are several individual saguaro cactus. They are spaced far apart, only four or five being visible in a several-mile stretch. These old saguaros are considered a "remnant" population, and there are no young cactus near them. Saguaros become common farther south in the Sonora Desert but are rare in the Mojave Desert.

Due to the great distances involved, we spent more than six weeks photographing in the Mojave Desert on several trips over many years. It was common to travel 140 miles or more to get to the area we wanted to photograph that day. We backpacked on several trips including one to Wild Horse Mesa at about 5,000 feet in altitude in the Providence Mountains. One of our favorite experiences was a boat trip on the Colorado River floating through Topock Gorge. The river in this gorge is untouched by man, with sheer rock walls and green water over 300 feet deep in places.

The Kelso Dunes (see title page) are the second-highest sand dunes in California, the Eureka Dunes in Death Valley National Monument being the tallest. We were at the Kelso Dunes during a time of very strong winds and bitter cold, near sunset. The sand was blowing off the top of the dunes, looking much like snow being blown off the summit of a mountain.

Natural arboretum.

Above: "The hats." (Beavertail cactus, early bloom.)
Opposite: Palm canyon, near Parker Dam.

Yucca spikes.

Colorado River, view towards Arizona in the vicinity of Topock Gorge.

Tidytips.

Winding through the goldfields.

Death Valley National Monument

Death Valley was given its name by one of the eighteen survivors of a party of thirty attempting to cross it in 1849. Within the valley lies the lowest point in the western hemisphere, near Badwater, at 282 feet below sea level. At Furnace Creek, not far from Badwater, summer temperatures regularly soar to 125 degrees Fahrenheit. The words "Death," "Badwater," and "Furnace," used in place names, are meant to strike fear in the heart for what can be extremely inhospitable environments. Borax deposits were found in 1873 and the famous image of 20-mule teams hauling this mineral out of Death Valley is a familiar one around the world. This romantic image of the early American West belies the tremendous difficulties of trying to live and work in these arid, hot conditions.

Death Valley National Monument was originally established in 1933. At that time it consisted of Death Valley and some of the bordering mountains. When the Desert Protection Act was passed in 1994, the original Death Valley Monument received National Park status. A large tract of adjacent desert, which included Eureka Valley and Eureka Dunes, was then added to Death Valley National Monument.

The stark, desert beauty of Death Valley attracts thousands of visitors each year, many coming from as far away as Asia and Europe. The area is especially popular in winter when the dry, sunny, and relatively comfortable temperatures are seen as a welcome change from the winter weather common in most of the northern hemisphere. Of the three Great American Deserts in this book, Death Valley is by far the most impacted by human visitors.

The topography of Death Valley National Monument ranges from low-lying salt flats that are the remains of ancient lakes to the rugged heights of the Panamint Mountains rising over 11,000 feet in the west. One of the most interesting features in the valley is the "Artist's Palette." Here green, pink, and white minerals have leached out of the ground. This is a naturally occurring phenomenon rather than the result of mining operations. The Death Valley dunes are another major landmark of the valley landscape.

Going over a small unnamed pass from California's Owens Valley the morning after a snowstorm, we were greeted by a Joshua tree forest covered in snow. What a delight! I have wanted to photograph Joshua trees in the snow for over twenty years, and here they were. We had to stop to take advantage of this unique opportunity.

The Eureka Dunes rise precipitously over 700 feet above the floor of Eureka Valley in a very remote, isolated, and starkly beautiful place. They are so unique that they are

Up the wash.

accorded special protection within California's Death Valley National Monument. They are the tallest dunes in California and the second-tallest in the U.S. These dunes are nothing like small seashore dunes. The breathtaking Eureka Dunes are like huge edifices with architectural elements reminiscent of the great Mayan pyramids of Central America.

The dunes are created by wind-blown particles from higher elevations in Eureka Valley. The wind creates swirling striations in the lower levels of the dunes—some of nature's abstract art—due in part to the difference in weight of the light- and dark-colored particles that make up the dunes. We were fortunate to be at Eureka Dunes during the full moon in the middle of winter. During this time of year the crystal clear air and the slanting light of winter create stunning visual drama. In the early morning and late afternoon when the angle of the sun is low, the shadows on the dunes create graceful sculptural curves. The massive structural elements of the dunes, the shadows, and the intricate two-tone swirls in the sand provide infinite visual interest and photographic possibilities.

Top, left: Rain splatters in the sand.

Bottom, left: Ghost cloud, Eureka Valley.

Death Valley Dunes.

Coastal Range

The redwood forests of the coastal range of central California are in the so-called "coastal rain forest." Part of the definition of a rain forest is that it receives 140 inches or more of rain per year. The coastal range of central California, however, averages 75 to 100 inches during approximately four months in winter and early spring. During this time the range exhibits all the characteristics of the great rain forests of the world. Verdant mosses and ferns abound. Trees and plants grow from old stumps and logs (called nurse logs) and springs gush forth from the ground.

The Santa Cruz Mountains of the central California coast are oriented north to south. Creeks that drain the west slope of the range empty directly into the Pacific Ocean. There are several streams that still support small salmon and steelhead runs, but all these waters are closed to fishing. There is little development north of the old whaling town of Davenport on the coast, and the water quality of the creeks is excellent.

The majestic redwood trees that grow in this range, *Sequoia sempervirens,* are well suited to the coastal humidity and near freezing wet winters. Another conifer native to the range is Douglas-fir. There are several varieties of oak, broadleaf maple, and madrone. Groves of whitish-barked western sycamore favor the wet soil adjacent to rivers and creeks.

This is my home range, and I have been privileged to photograph it for many years through all the seasons. Badger Springs is on the east fork of Soquel Creek deep in the Soquel Demonstration State Forest. I have photographed here "in the round," that is through all the seasons of the year. Images from Badger Springs are included showing fall, winter, and spring foliage.

Above: Female Allen hummingbird.
Opposite: Maple leaves with catkins.

Fall

There is a common notion that people living in the coastal regions of California don't see much seasonal change. However, many things occur in the coastal forests of the Santa Cruz Mountains that indicate the approach of the fall season. The first and very noticeable color change actually happens in late summer. At this time the poison oak vine has a color palette of rich reds and oranges. Its beauty rivals that of any of nature's fall color shows.

Bigleaf maple, being deciduous throughout its range, drops all its leaves each year. Before the leaves fall to the ground, they turn wonderful shades of brilliant yellow and rusty orange. Their catkin-like seed pods turn black and open to drop the seeds. Bigleaf maples growing near stream banks provide a startling burst of color in the deep shade and greenery of the forest.

The toyon or Christmas berry shrub grows beneath the redwood canopy. Toyon is the official California state shrub. Clusters of drooping white flowers turn into clusters of bright red berries in late November and early December. These berries, as the name "Christmas berry shrub" imply, stay fresh until well after Christmas.

The evergreen redwood and Douglas-fir shed only their dead, dry needles each fall. The madrone, a hardwood, is also evergreen throughout its range. However, some of the old leaves on the madrone do change color and eventually fall to the ground. These older leaves display bright gradations of red, yellow, and green (a different hue of green than the young leaves). Madrone also produces reddish orange berries that, like the toyon, last well into the start of the new year.

Opposite: Poison oak.

Toyon berries.

Reflections in Soquel Creek.

Above: Bigleaf maples along Soquel Creek.
Opposite: "Fallen, but still beautiful." (Soquel Creek.)

Winter

Winter is the time when the coastal range comes alive. For up to seven months a year it is deprived of moisture except for coastal fog. Rainwater is the lifeblood of the forest. The ground becomes saturated and water starts to run off. Creeks rise and springs gush forth from the sides of slopes. It is the time of renewal, much the way spring is in climates that have protracted winter freezes. Mosses that have been flat, brown, and dormant become shades of vivid green and when viewed up close resemble the trees in the forest of which they are a part. They stand up like little trees.

All the photographs made during the winter season were shot while it was raining, most at the height of storms. These images evoke an emotional response from me based on my memories of the sound of wind and rushing water, the feeling of the rain, and the extraordinary visual tapestry of the many shades of green.

Natural Bridges State Park is part of Monterey Bay, on the west side of the city of Santa Cruz. The eucalyptus grove in the park is the wintering grounds of large swarms of monarch butterflies. They are bright orange with patterns of black and are called by some "flying gems." They hang from the eucalyptus branches in clusters that look like large flower blossoms. The monarch migration follows the bloom cycle of the milkweed plant. The larvae feed on the milkweed and accumulate a poisonous alkaloid compound that makes them distasteful. Birds have learned to recognize the monarch's bright color pattern and avoid eating them. The summer range of monarchs extends through the northwest of the United States and up into Canada. The monarchs that leave Natural Bridges for their summer migration north are not the same generation that returns the following winter. The monarchs that arrive at the wintering grounds have never been there before. Somehow the knowledge of where to go is imprinted on them by the preceding generation.

Up the coast from Natural Bridges, a short distance from the old whaling town of Davenport, is Año Nuevo State Reserve. Año Nuevo is home to the largest mainland breeding colony of elephant seals in the world. The elephant seal was so-named because the bull's nose looks like a short version of an elephant's trunk. The breeding season is from December to March. The mature bulls are an incredible 14 to 16 feet long and can easily weigh 5,000 pounds. The bulls engage in violent battles to gain breeding rights. The breeding bulls establish and then vigorously defend their harems. Within six days of arriving, the females give birth to the pups that were conceived here the previous winter. When these pups are weaned at four to six weeks old, their original coat of black fur starts to molt and is replaced by a shiny, silver-hued coat. These unbelievably cute pups are called "weaners" at this stage of their development.

Opposite: Tree moss during storm, Badger Springs.

Above: "Old and new." (Badger Springs.)
Opposite: Monarch butterflies, Natural Bridges State Park.

Sycamore trees and iridescent green moss on stream boulders.

Deep forest oaks during a big winter storm.

Above: Big bull elephant seal.

Right: Elephant seal nuptials.

Redwoods in the fog.

California poppies.

WILD ORCHIDS

Of the three orchids shown on pages 68 and 69, the Rein orchid is uncommon to rare, the spotted coralroot is uncommon, and the western coralroot is uncommon to common. All are terrestrial in nature, having roots in the ground. The coralroots, which are saprophytes, grow from decaying organic matter without photosynthesis. All grow in an environment that, except for fog, gets no moisture during the growing season.

The Rein orchid grows as a single slender stem 18 to 24 inches tall with 30 to 40 blooms on the stem. Growth starts with a single pair of leaves near the ground, which turn brown and whither before the blooms form. The blooms are small, about $1/2$ inch with their tails. Conditions have to be completely to their liking for the Rein orchid to bloom, and the blooms last almost two months.

Left: Spotted coralroot.

Below: Western coralroot.

The coralroots tend to grow in clusters, and rarely repeat growing in the same location. Sometimes several years go by without seeing them in proximity to where they were before. They grow about ten inches in height, and the blooms inhabit the upper portion of the stems. Their reddish brown stems grow without leaves, hence producing no chlorophyll.

Bush lupine.

"Primavera." (Douglas-fir needles, first spring growth.)

Mountains and Valleys

When viewed from the air, it is easy to see why the Sierra Nevada mountains of California are often considered the spine of the state. The approximately 70-mile-wide range is a huge uplifted fault running north and south for over 400 miles. The highest point in the range, Mount Whitney, is also the highest point in California at 14,495 feet in altitude. These photographs of the Sierras are all from the escarpment, or east side of the range.

The Sierras contain many diverse biological areas. Images of the southern Sierra in Sequoia National Forest actually include both desert and alpine zones from sites within a distance of about fifty miles. Arranged geographically from south to north, our images also include historic Mono Lake with its tufa towers, the Bodie ghost town, and the Toiyabe National Forest in the vicinity of Sonora Pass

Above: *Nose Ridge, Twin Lakes Road.*
Opposite: *Curving road, west Walker River.*

Southern Sequoia

The southern Sequoia National Forest is an area of great bio-diversity. It encompasses pure alpine, mixed, and desert zones. The alpine zone has mixed conifers growing on relatively steep terrain with many water courses, the main water course being the Kern River. The mixed zone contains diverse plant combinations such as owl clover pastures with cholla cactus. The desert terrain has forests of Joshua trees. It is amazing that these very diverse zones are within about 40 miles of one another. Conifer trees and Joshua trees growing in such close proximity is truly unique.

This is a fabulous place for spring wildflowers! During the El Nino spring of 1998, there was a profusion of wildflowers carpeting the ground, and our images were photographed during that wonderful season. The colors were so intense and there was so much in bloom that it was sometimes difficult to decide what to photograph. As a mentor of mine once pointed out, film is the cheapest thing you take to the field—so shoot a lot of it! I did just that.

Our images are from southern Sequoia National Forest—not to be confused with Sequoia National Park (within the National Forest)—which is on the west slope of the Sierra Nevada. Southern Sequoia National Forest is in southeastern Kern County. The Piute Mountains to the south of Lake Isabella and particularly Kelso Valley are the sites of many of the photographs of mixed and desert zones. Most of the images of the alpine zone were shot along Cannell Creek which drains into the Kern River northeast of the town of Kernville and Lake Isabella.

Lone Joshua tree.

Joshua tree bloom.

Indian paintbrush, before sunrise.

Above: Owl clover.
Opposite: Field of filaree.

Mono Lake

Eerie, surreal, otherworldly, and just plain weird are all terms that describe the tufa (pronounced "toofah") towers of Mono Lake. These towers are spectacular examples of what nature can create with only a few ingredients. The unusual spires found here form when calcium-bearing fresh water bubbles up in an alkaline lake rich in carbonates. The limestone pinnacles are made by the precipitation of the combined calcium and carbonate. This process is similar to the formation of stalagmites and stalactites in a cave. The reaction only happens underwater. As the water level in the lake drops, the exposed towers cease to grow. The towers at Mono Lake are estimated to be between 200 and 900 years old.

The lake itself, one of the oldest in North America, is over 700,000 years old. Over millennia salts and minerals have washed down into the lake from Eastern Sierra streams. Freshwater evaporating from the lake has concentrated the level of salts so that now Mono Lake is over two and one half times as salty and eighty times as alkaline as seawater.

As little as 100 years ago Mono Lake was large enough to be used for ferry transport. Ferries went north from the town of Lee Vining on the West shore to near the old mining town of Bodie. Water level marks are visible on the hills adjacent to the dirt road that goes to Bodie.

These show that there were relatively long periods of water-level stability during the gradual decline of the level of the lake. Today Bodie is a ghost town, the viable mineral wealth having been played out long ago.

In 1941 the city of Los Angeles began diverting water from streams that feed Mono Lake, and the water level dropped over 40 feet. This use of water from the Owens Valley and Mono Lake's feeder streams is the theme of the famous movie *Chinatown*. In 1994, after many years of legal maneuvering, an order was issued that protects Mono Lake and its tributary streams. This action will raise the level of the lake by 17 feet over the next twenty years. Mono Lake is now a state reserve protected within the Mono Basin National Forest Scenic Area. It was a pleasure to photograph a wild place where the ecology is improving rather than declining due to human pressures.

While Mono Lake has been called a "dead sea," this is not the case. Few animals can tolerate the salty, alkaline water of the lake, but creatures abound in the trillions! Half-inch-long brine shrimp can be seen in Mono Lake from April through October. The shrimp provide an abundant food supply for more than eighty species of migratory birds.

Opposite: Tufa towers and approaching storm.

Left: Tufa reflections.

Below: Tufa landscape.

Shore grasses.

Bodie

In 1859 Waterman S. Body and Black Taylor came upon what was to become one of the richest gold discoveries the west had ever known. A town named Body soon sprang up in this high desert valley. The spelling of the name of the town was later changed to "Bodie" to avoid mispronunciation. Body himself never enjoyed the fruits of his discovery. He froze to death while attempting to bring supplies back to town during his first winter there.

In 1877 the Standard Mining Company made an extremely rich gold and silver strike, and the boom was on. In its heyday Bodie was known as the most lawless, wildest, and toughest mining camp the far west had ever known. The boom cycle didn't last long, and after 1882 much of the town was abandoned. The town suffered two fires. The last, in 1932, destroyed all but the 10 percent of the town remaining today. Bodie was designated a National Historic Site and State Historic Park in 1962 and is preserved in a state of arrested decay. The first time I was in Bodie was over twenty five years ago. The last time I was there was in 2001. Much to the credit of the conservators, not much had changed.

One of the most interesting features of Bodie is the glass in the windows of the buildings. In those frames that have the original windows, the glass is wavy. At the time this historic glass was manufactured, the technology didn't exist for making the perfectly flat glass of today. As I looked at these windows and saw the wavy reflections, I felt eerily connected to the past and the people who had lived here.

Opposite: Tattered lace.

Above: Old wagon wheel.

Right: "Meals from the past."
(Window reflection.)

Town at sunset.

Eerie reflections.

Toiyabe National Forest

Coming east down from the Sonora Pass on the escarpment side of the Sierras, one of the first breathtaking views is of the West Walker River as it flows through Leavitt Meadow and adjacent Pickel Meadow. When I first came upon this vista, my immediate thought was "this is what a wild valley should look like in the great American west." The grand landscapes in all the western movies ever made are embodied here.

I was introduced to this area over 35 years ago as a student at a survival school run by the United States Marine Corps. I went to courses here in both summer and winter. Nighttime temperatures here reach minus 20 degrees Fahrenheit. During one of my courses at the survival school, I heard and saw my first mountain lion. The lion woke me up with its uncanny yell, and as I opened my eyes, I saw that it was only about twenty feet away! I loved the school, and the area. I have returned here many times over the years to smell the pristine air, feel the solitude of nature, and see and photograph the beauty of the place.

Aspen groves are plentiful here, especially on slopes that drain into streams. Silver Creek, which flows into the west Walker River, is no exception. The unbelievable yellow of the fall aspen leaves dazzles the eye when struck by the first morning sun rays. At an elevation around 7,500 feet above sea level, the color of the sky, rich in ultra violet light, is a vibrant primary blue.

Opposite: Yellow aspen leaves at sunrise.

Alpine meadow above west Walker River.

Wildlife Refuges

What is being done on the Klamath Basin Wildlife Refuges (KWR) seems a noble use of our tax dollars. Six National Wildlife Refuges managed by the U.S. Fish and Wildlife Service have been established in the basin. Approximately one-third of the total refuge acreage is leased to farmers for the production of cereal grains. Each of these leases contains a proviso for leaving a significant portion of the grain fallow in the fields to attract migrating bird populations. Over 75 percent of the Pacific Flyway waterfowl pass through the refuges. Peak late fall concentrations are regularly over one million birds.

Above: Tundra swan warms wings in morning sunlight.
Opposite: Tundra swans over Mount Shasta.

Lower Klamath Lake and Tule Lake, both entirely within the state of California, are the focus of this section. Lower Klamath Lake Refuge, established by President Theodore Roosevelt, was our country's first waterfowl refuge. We spent three years working at KWR. By mid fall, large concentrations of Canada geese were already present, and snow geese were just arriving. After Thanksgiving, most of the Canadas were gone, replaced by hundreds of thousands of snow and white front geese. The first year we made the post-Thanksgiving trip, the Klamath Basin received over 15 inches of snow. Almost all the geese were gone within two days because their food was covered with snow. During the end-of-January trip each year, in bitter-cold weather with snow on the ground, we photographed bald eagles and tundra swans. KWR has the largest migrating population of bald eagles in the lower 48 states.

These images cannot convey the enveloping sensory experience of sight and sound when tens of thousands of geese take off at the same time. The cacophony of sounds as the flock makes ready to fly, followed by the unbelievable drumming of the air their wings make as they take off, is extraordinary.

Lower Klamath Lake

Near the end of January the surface water in the refuges is frozen but for a few open leads. Early morning temperatures hover around zero, and the days warm up to the mid-twenties. We are here because bald eagles are here—a lot of bald eagles! The biologist at KWR estimated that there were between 400 and 500 eagles at the refuges during our first visit. They were mostly concentrated on Lower Klamath Lake. We repeatedly saw over 100 at a time, sighting over 1000 eagles in five days in the field! It is a real success story that a previously endangered bird has recovered so well.

The eagles, in their tuxedo-like plumage, ringed the open leads in the ice and watched the ducks and geese for signs of weakness, picking off those too slow to evade them. They are called the "Undertakers." Avian cholera, introduced to KWR in the mid-1940s, brought the eagles. Until then, few bald eagles wintered here. They are not susceptible to this form of avian cholera, but their prey here is. As the word spread through the Alaskan eagle population, KWR became the-place-to-be for winter feeding. The bald eagle belongs to the fish eagle group. We all have the mental image of this majestic bird swooping down to the surface of a pristine alpine lake and snatching a gleaming trout in its talons. For the eagles to eat like they do at KWR is learned behavior.

Almost all the ducks and geese flew away when a big snow storm hit just after Thanksgiving, covering their food. Needless to say, we were concerned that because of the exodus of the waterfowl from KWR, the eagles might not come. Not so! Again they demonstrated their adaptability and changed their eating habits. The cereal grain leases on the refuges are prepared for spring planting in much the same manner as rice; the fields are flooded in winter. The Bureau of Reclamation is responsible for flooding the fields, and in a wonderful act of wildlife management cooperation, the biologists at KWR coordinate with the Bureau of Reclamation to flood the fields slowly. This forces the rodents, many thousands of them, to abandon their burrows and gives the eagles an alternate food source.

One afternoon we observed an adult eagle fly, really sort of jump, to a spot in a field and come up with a rodent in his beak. After consuming this rodent, he stood quietly and watched the ground. In the course of the next ten minutes, he reached with his beak and caught at least five more rodents. We named him the "Chief Hunter." As a result of his activities, two crows and a seagull came over hoping to scavenge his leavings. The bald eagle is truly at the top of the food chain, and the "Chief Hunter" merely looked at these upstarts with what we thought to be amused disdain. The scavengers didn't stand a chance!

Blackbirds roost for the night.

There were over 100 eagles feeding in this field at the time. We were so amazed that all these eagles showed up at once, we named the field "Eagle dot com."

Traveling along a snow-covered dike looking for eagles, we heard a great commotion of sounds similar to those of a flock of geese. Puzzled because there were virtually no geese on the refuge, we continued toward the sound. We stopped when we could see a lot of movement in a previously flooded—now frozen—field. Through binoculars the movement on the ice was seen to be tundra swans, thousands of tundra swans! They were a surprise. This was the start of their northern spring migration. These magnificent birds allowed us an unusually close approach. As it turned out, the swans were at the refuge each January of our three annual trips.

Tundra swans are huge! Their wingspans are over seven feet, and an adult weighs approximately twenty pounds. Watching them walk on ice was very humorous; in spite of having significant "claws" at the end of each toe of their webbed feet, they slipped frequently. This cartoon-like sliding and falling on the ice contrasted greatly with their gracefulness in flight.

"Eagle dot com." (Many eagles feed in a field near Lower Klamath Lake.)

Tundra swans take off from the ice.

FOOD FIGHTS!

Scouting the north side of Lower Klamath Lake during the midwinter visit of our third year, we observed what appeared to be a group of crows in the air and on the ice squabbling over a carcass. As our car sped by this scene, my spouse started shouting at me to stop and back up. "They're eagles," she cried! There were six mature bald eagles whirling around, with two or three on the ice at any one time. The fuss was over a duck carcass that had been frozen in the lake ice the previous night. Any one of these birds was capable of fly- ing away with a duck in its talons. What kept them all here was they couldn't get the carcass free from the ice. For the next several hours we were treated to their very humorous antics. Once again the accepted image of the eagle with the gleaming trout in its talons was altered.

Above: "I'm not impressed."

Left: Food fight.

Left: "Who goes first?"

Below: "It's mine!"

Flyback wing.

Sandhill cranes.

Canada geese in flight.

Coyote stalks geese.

Moonrise over Lower Klamath Lake.

Tule Lake

The migrating geese here are part of the gigantic Pacific Flyway. They are truly wild, and because hunting is permitted on some portions of the refuge, they are extremely wary of human approach. To overcome this we spent the latter part of the afternoons scouting locations where we expected the geese to overnight. In the morning we would be in place before first light to minimize the effects of our presence. In early November this meant sitting almost motionless with temperatures just below freezing. Frequently during our post-Thanksgiving trip, early morning temperatures were in the 'teens with snow on the ground.

Our work quickly fell into rhythm with the birds' feeding patterns. Right before sunrise and for about an hour after, flocks would fly out to the surrounding grain fields for their morning feeding. The flyouts were by individual flocks. The midmorning flybacks were a different story. Massive wings of thousands of geese each were arrayed across the sky, one after the other. Day after day they flew back to the refuge this way. They were first visible as they crossed a low range of hills about eight miles north of Tule Lake. We frequently heard them before they were visible to us. Sometimes there were seven or eight flyback wings visible at the same time. Because they were traversing hunting areas, the flybacks maintained an altitude well above gun range. Only when they were over the area

where they wanted to land would the geese perform incredible aerial maneuvers to lose altitude precipitously and land on the lake. The same pattern was repeated in the late afternoon. We did not photograph the evening flyback, as this occurs well after dark. These feeding patterns continued for as long as there were geese on the refuge and were the same regardless of species.

The early November trip was predominately sightings of Canada geese. Toward the end of the first week, small numbers—less than 100—of snow geese started to show up. We witnessed the remarkable phenomenon of ten to twenty snow geese leading a flyback wing of thousands of Canada geese. The snows did not fly out with the Canadas and did not land in the same place as the Canadas when they returned to the lake. When we returned after Thanksgiving, almost all the Canada geese were gone, replaced by snow and white front geese.

Sometime in the first few days of December, we were treated to an extraordinary sight: tundra swans (formerly known as whistling swans). As we watched, a skein of 55 of these huge birds took off and slowly flew upwind right in front of us. During one bitter-cold sunrise, with a harsh wind blowing, we were treated to viewing a mated pair of swans flying in front of Mt. Shasta!

Predawn takeoff, Canada geese.

The sunlight before dark.

Right: "Ghost birds." (Canada geese.)

Below: Snow geese wedge.

Sacramento National Wildlife Refuge

We were given the gift of perfect timing during our narrow window of opportunity to be at the Sacramento National Wildlife Refuge. Due to early snow in the northern portion of the flyway, snow geese were packed into this refuge. The biologist told us the count for snow geese alone was almost 100,000 birds! We were there at the peak of the season.

We were frequently treated to the experience of 25,000 or more snow geese taking to the air at once during our morning field sessions. They literally roared into the air, so loud was the sound of their wings. In other refuges we had worked on, we were able to discern the pattern of the geese and swans' feeding flights, but these snow geese were unpredictable. We could not figure out why these huge gaggles were taking to the air. The biologist assured us that even though we could see no predator spooking them, there had to be at least one responsible for their "blowing up" off the refuge. They often repeated this phenomenon four or five times in a single morning.

The Sacramento National Wildlife Refuge is part of a complex consisting of six different refuges. Prior to the introduction of agriculture, the majority of the Sacramento Valley existed as seasonal wetlands and grasslands. Millions of waterfowl migrated down the Pacific Flyway to winter in the valley. With natural habitat lost, the refuges were established to conserve the flyway, attracting the waterfowl to specific areas by creating suitable habitat and food sources. The first of the six refuges was established during the depression by the Civilian Conservation Corps; the last of the six was completed almost 50 years later. All are almost entirely man-made. As the natural wetlands were diverted for agriculture, the water habitats on all six refuges were created by man. The six refuges in the complex provide a significant amount of the wintering habitat for waterfowl in the Sacramento Valley. As is the case for all the NWRs we worked on, the refuges play a major role in protecting the birds of the Pacific Flyway.

"Full flaps." (Immature snow goose.)

Above: Slow-speed takeoff, snow geese.

Left: Snow geese take off in the fog.

Gaggle of snow geese take to the air.

Crowded landing area, snow geese.

Overleaf: "A bizzilion snow geese."

Volcano!

Mount Shasta is part of the Cascade Range. The Cascade Range is a string of volcanic peaks starting with Mount Lassen south of Mount Shasta and continuing into British Columbia. Mount Rainier in Washington state is part of this range. All volcanic peaks of the Cascade Range are part of the Pacific "Ring of Fire."

Canadian fur trader Peter Skene Ogden is credited with discovering the mountain in the early 1800s, although Indians lived there for at least hundreds of years prior to that. The first recorded climb of Mount Shasta was in the mid-1800s. The Museum of the Siskyous has photographs of some interesting early attempts to climb the mountain. Amazing photographs of one of these early ascents shows that horses were used and some actually made it to the summit. Women in bustles riding side saddle and carrying parasols were actually part of this climb.

According to the U.S. Geological Survey, Mount Shasta is an active volcano, although dormant—for the time being. It is the second most active volcano in the Cascade Range and the most active volcano in California. It last erupted in 1786 and has erupted approximately every 300 years. There is an active sulphur fumarole in a shallow caldera near the summit, at around 14,000 feet. Sulfuric gasses bubble through a small vent in the mountain creating a hot spring almost three feet in diameter.

Mount Shasta has permanent glaciers on its flanks from northwest to northeast. While the south side of the mountain receives more snow, it also faces the sun, resulting in great frozen snow fields but no permanent glaciers.

Above: *Conifer after winter storm.*
Opposite: *Glacial serac, Bolam Glacier.*

Bolam Glacier

Establishing a base camp on the terminal moraine of Bolam Glacier on the northwest side of the mountain was a demanding undertaking. It involved driving up the mountain via difficult four-wheel-drive tracks for over ten miles. We then proceeded on foot to above the tree line, and finally climbed a scree-filled chute to our campsite at 11,300 feet in altitude. From here we could see the top of Bolam Glacier and the summit of the mountain over four and one half miles away. Getting to base camp was strenuous enough to require spending two nights resting and becoming acclimatized to the altitude before attempting any serious climbing on the glacier.

To me, the most beautiful place on the mountain is Bolam Glacier, a three- to four-story-high serac wall several miles up the glacier. A serac forms when the ice, in its downward movement, cannot flow over a steep underlying slope and breaks, leaving a vertical wall with a jumbled ice field below. The wall has horizontal layers of green and white ice, much the same as annual rings on a tree. From these layers climatologists are able to study past weather patterns.

Tales abound of unexplainable sights and sounds on Mount Shasta. There are legends of a group of super-beings, the Lemurians, who are said to live deep within the mountain. The legend of St. Germaine is also part of the moun-

tain's lore. St. Germaine is said to have appeared to travelers as a black panther on the slopes below Avalanche Gulch, and Panther Meadows is named in honor of this legend. Earlier in this century many people traveling by train saw lights on the northwest side of the mountain. In the winter, with snow on the trees, the tinkling of many glass bells has been heard by thousands of people.

I, and my partners, have seen the eerie and beautiful lights and heard the bells on many occasions at different areas of the mountain. The most notable phenomenon occurred at evening twilight at our base camp on the terminal moraine of Bolam Glacier. We had finished dinner and gotten undressed and into our sleeping bags. Alas, I found I had to brave the cold to relieve myself. When I got out of my tent, the entire serac wall appeared as if it were illuminated by fluorescent lights—from within! I called to my partners, exhorting them to come out of their tents and look at the wall. As it was below freezing, they thought I was trying to play a joke on them. It took a lot of cajoling to get them out of their sleeping bags. Eventually all four of us stood gazing in awe at the spectacle. Of course we tried to come up with logical explanations, but failed.

Mount Shasta is truly one of the magical places on our planet.

Opposite: Four miles to the summit.

Right: View from the summit.

Below: Looking up Avalanch Gulch.

The Photography

Photography has been used as a medium for chronicling California's wilderness since before the gold rush days. The individual responsible, in my opinion, for elevating this photographic venue to an art form was Ansel Adams. His stunning images of California forever changed the way natural history photographs are viewed.

Ansel Adams was known for his use of large format cameras with negative sizes of 8 by 10 inches and greater. These large bulky cameras were required to achieve first rate images with the technology available to him at the time. Today's technology of cameras, lenses, lights, and film make it possible to go to the field with considerably smaller and lighter equipment.

Both Hasselblad medium format and Nikon 35mm equipment were used to produce these images, depending on application. For my underwater work I used Nikon 35mm equipment exclusively. My lens of choice for most of the work was a 15mm Nikkor corrected for underwater use mounted on a Nikonos 5 camera. I also used a housed Nikon with a macro lens for the really close shots. All of the underwater work was lighted with multiple strobes, frequently with the help of an assistant handholding a third off-camera strobe. At the complete opposite end of the focal length scale, many of the images shot on national wildlife refuges were made using a 400mm

lens and a doubler, making the focal length 800 mm. The effective magnification is approximately sixteen power. This arrangement was used to capture the images of bald eagles and other migratory waterfowl. At times two strobes were mounted atop the lens to enhance the detail of the birds.

Virtually all of the landscape work was done in medium format using Hasselblad equipment. The larger image size, which is over three times larger than 35mm, produces wonderful detail. My camera body of choice for many of the landscapes was a Hasselblad flex body. This body has a bellows which allows the lens mount to be tilted. Tilting the lens mount makes it possible to achieve greater sharpness throughout the image.

The images were made in almost every conceivable environment on the planet and in various weather conditions. Rain, snow, below-zero temperatures, temperatures in excess of 100 degrees Fahrenheit, and underwater environments were all part of the photographic adventure. The care and treatment of batteries was critical to the work. In extreme cold, we kept spare battery packs inside our parkas. These were swapped with the cold in-camera batteries on a regular basis to keep the equipment functioning.

Technology is just one aspect of the photographic work represented here. The best images were shot when my familiarity with the technology being used—both the photographic and environmental equipment—allowed me to forget about technical particulars when composing images. With nothing intruding on the creative process, the results are always better than when I am concerned with some technical detail

Range fence, Sweetwater Valley, Bridgeport, California.